A Dog's Life

Also edited by Lee Bennett Hopkins

HEY-HOW FOR HALLOWEEN!

SING HEY FOR CHRISTMAS DAY!

GOOD MORNING TO YOU, VALENTINE

BEAT THE DRUM: INDEPENDENCE DAY HAS COME

MERRILY COMES OUR HARVEST IN: POEMS FOR THANKSGIVING

EASTER BUDS ARE SPRINGING: POEMS FOR EASTER

TO LOOK AT ANY THING

MY MANE CATCHES THE WIND: POEMS ABOUT HORSES

MOMENTS: POEMS ABOUT THE SEASONS

I AM THE CAT

RAINBOWS ARE MADE: POEMS BY CARL SANDBURG

A Dog's Life

POEMS SELECTED BY LEE BENNETT HOPKINS

Illustrated by Linda Rochester Richards

HARCOURT BRACE JOVANOVICH, PUBLISHERS

SAN DIEGO   NEW YORK   LONDON

LIBRARY OF CONGRESS CATALOGING IN PUBLICATION DATA
Main entry under title: A Dog's life.
SUMMARY: A collection of twenty-three poems celebrating one of man's best friends, the dog.
  1. Dogs—Juvenile poetry. 2. Children's poetry, American. [1. Dogs—Poetry. 2. American poetry—Collections]
I. Hopkins, Lee Bennett. II. Richards, Linda Rochester, ill.
PS595.D63D6   811'.008'036   82-974
ISBN 0-15-223937-5

FIRST EDITION   B C D E

Every effort has been made to trace the ownership of all copyrighted material and to secure the necessary permissions to reprint these selections. In the event of any question arising as to the use of any material, the editor and publisher, while expressing regret for any inadvertent error, will be happy to make the necessary correction in future printings.

Thanks are due to the following for permission to reprint the copyrighted materials listed below:

ATHENEUM PUBLISHERS, INC., for "Old Dog" by Patricia Hubbell in Catch Me a Wind. Copyright © 1968 by Patricia Hubbell (New York: Atheneum, 1968); for "For Mugs" by Myra Cohn Livingston in 4-Way Stop and Other Poems. Copyright © 1976 by Myra Cohn Livingston. A Margaret K. McElderry book (New York: Atheneum, 1976); and for "Making a Friend" by Myra Cohn Livingston in O Sliver of Liver. Copyright © 1979 by Myra Cohn Livingston. A Margaret K. McElderry book (New York: Atheneum, 1979). All reprinted with the permission of Atheneum Publishers, Inc.

THOMAS Y. CROWELL PUBLISHERS for "A Dog" from River Winding by Charlotte Zolotow. Copyright © 1970 by Charlotte Zolotow. Reprinted by permission of Thomas Y. Crowell Publishers.

CURTIS BROWN, LTD., for "Autumn" from the poem, "The Seasons," by Harry Behn in Chrysalis. Copyright © 1968 by Harry Behn; for "Hansi" by Harry Behn from The Golden Hive. Copyright © 1966 by Harry Behn; and for "Puppy" by Lee Bennett Hopkins. Copyright © 1974 by Lee Bennett Hopkins. All reprinted by permission of Curtis Brown, Ltd.

DOUBLEDAY & COMPANY, INC., for "Pete at the Seashore" from The Lives and Times of Archy and Mehitabel by Don Marquis. Copyright 1935 by Doubleday & Company, Inc. Reprinted by permission of the publisher.

FARRAR, STRAUS & GIROUX, INC., for "Dog" from Small Poems by Valerie Worth. Text copyright © 1972 by Valerie Worth. Reprinted by permission of Farrar, Straus & Giroux, Inc.

THE GOLDEN QUILL PRESS and MARSHALL JONES COMPANY, PUBLISHERS, for "Puppy" by Robert L. Tyler from The Deposition of Don Quixote and Other Poems.

HARCOURT BRACE JOVANOVICH, INC., for "Dan" from Smoke and Steel by Carl Sandburg, copyright 1920 by Harcourt Brace Jovanovich, Inc.; copyright 1948 by Carl Sandburg. Reprinted by permission of the publisher.

HARPER & ROW, PUBLISHERS, INC., for "Familiar Friends" from Crickety Cricket! The Best Loved Poems of James S. Tippett. Copyright 1930 by Harper & Row, Publishers, Inc.; renewed 1958 by James S. Tippett; for "Full of the Moon" from Dogs & Dragon Trees & Dreams by Karla Kuskin. Copyright © 1958 by Karla Kuskin; and for "Vern" from Bronzeville Boys and Girls by Gwendolyn Brooks. Copyright © 1956 by Gwendolyn Brooks Blakely. All reprinted by permission of Harper & Row, Publishers, Inc.

HOLT, RINEHART AND WINSTON, PUBLISHERS, for "The Span of Life" from The Poetry of Robert Frost edited by Edward Connery Lathem. Copyright 1936 by Robert Frost. Copyright © 1964 by Lesley Frost Ballantine. Copyright © 1969 by Holt, Rinehart and Winston. Reprinted by permission of Holt, Rinehart and Winston, Publishers.

BERTHA KLAUSNER INTERNATIONAL LITERARY AGENCY, INC., for "To Sup Like a Pup" from I Would Like to Be a Pony by Dorothy W. Baruch. Permission granted by the Bertha Klausner International Literary Agency.

J. B. LIPPINCOTT PUBLISHERS for 19 lines from "Friend Dog" by Arnold Adoff. Copyright © 1980 by Arnold Adoff. Reprinted by permission of J. B. Lippincott Publishers.

LITTLE, BROWN AND COMPANY for "Gone" from One at a Time: His Collected Poems for the Young by David McCord. © 1970 by David McCord. By permission of Little, Brown and Company.

LOUIS PHILLIPS for "Dream Dog." Used by permission of the author who controls all rights.

LOUISE H. SCLOVE for "The Ambiguous Dog" from Lyric Laughter by Arthur Guiterman. Copyright 1939 by E. P. Dutton, Inc. Reprinted by permission of Louise H. Sclove.

VIKING PENGUIN INC. for "Prayer of the Dog" from Prayers from the Ark by Carmen Bernos de Gasztold, translated by Rumer Godden. English text copyright ©1962 by Rumer Godden; for the second stanza of "The Old Dog's Song" from Merlin and the Snake's Egg by Leslie Norris. Copyright © 1978 by Leslie Norris; and for "Lone Dog" from Songs to Save a Soul by Irene Rutherford McLeod. All reprinted by permission of Viking Penguin, Inc.

For
Wanda Lee Schumacher,
Lover of Life

Contents

Introduction

Poets sing of everything.

In this book, you will meet poets
who have sung the praises of dogs, depicting them in a
variety of actions and moods and in various stages of
life, from frisky, playful puppies to aging dogs.

The very first animal to be domesticated, dogs
have been treasured pets for centuries and have inspired
poets from England, France, and rural and urban America.

Meet these poets and their songs in *A Dog's Life*.

Lee Bennett Hopkins
SCARBOROUGH, NEW YORK

Puppy
LEE BENNETT HOPKINS

We bought our puppy
   A brand new bed
But he likes sleeping
   On mine instead.

And I'm glad he does
   'Cause I'd miss his cold nose
Waking me up
   Tickling my toes.

To Sup Like a Pup

DOROTHY W. BARUCH

To sup
Like a pup,
To gulp it all up
No napkin
No fork
No spoon
And no cup
But to slup
With your tongue
In dee-lish-able laps . . .
What luck!

Vern
GWENDOLYN BROOKS

When walking in a tiny rain
Across a vacant lot,
A pup's a good companion—
If a pup you've got.

And when you've had a scold,
And no one loves you very,
And you cannot be merry,
A pup will let you look at him,
And even let you hold
His little wiggly warmness—

And let you snuggle down beside.
Nor mock the tears you have to hide.

Dan

CARL SANDBURG

Early May, after cold rain the sun baffling cold wind.
Irish setter pup finds a corner near the cellar door,
                 all sun and no wind,
Cuddling there he crosses forepaws and lays his skull
Sideways on this pillow, dozing in a half-sleep,
Browns of hazel nut, mahogany, rosewood, played off
                 against each other on his paws
                 and head.

Puppy
ROBERT L. TYLER

Catch and shake the cobra garden hose.
Scramble on panicky paws and flee
The hiss of tensing nozzle nose,
Or stalk that snobbish bee.

The back yard world is vast as park
With belly-tickle grass and stun
Of sudden sprinkler squalls that are
Rainbows to the yap yap sun.

16

The Ambiguous Dog

ARTHUR GUITERMAN

The dog beneath the cherry-tree
Has ways that sorely puzzle me:

Behind, he wags a friendly tail;
Before, his growl would turn you pale!

His meaning isn't plain and clear;
Oh, is the wag or growl sincere?

I think I'd better not descend;
His bite is at the growly end.

17

He wouldn't come at first.
But when
I stood quite still a long time,
Then

His tail began to move.
His eyes
Looked into mine, and in
Surprise

He sort of sniffed and showed
His tongue.
Then, suddenly, he moved and
Sprung

To where I stood. He smelled
My feet
And came up close so we could
Meet.

So then, I gently stroked
His head.
"Good boy—I'll be your friend,"
I said.

He licked me then, and that
Was good,
Because it meant
He understood.

Making a Friend
MYRA COHN LIVINGSTON

Hansi

HARRY BEHN

Our dog is not stupid, but stubborn, and so
He simply refuses to notice or know
What anyone else can easily see,
That there's an owl in the tulip tree,
   A big owl blinking its yellow eyes,
   Turning its head, and looking wise.

But Hansi simply refuses to care
To look in a tree to see what's there.
We point and shout and whatever we say
He just turns more the other way.
   It's different, though, when out he goes
   Each morning to read the news with his nose!

19

Dream Dog
LOUIS PHILLIPS

Dream dog leaps out of the moon with nothing
  in its muzzle but bones of yellow light.

20

Lone Dog
IRENE RUTHERFORD McLEOD

I'm a lean dog, a keen dog, a wild dog, and lone;
I'm a rough dog, a tough dog, hunting on my own!
I'm a bad dog, a mad dog, teasing silly sheep;
I love to sit and bay the moon, to keep fat souls from sleep.

I'll never be a lap dog, licking dirty feet,
A sleek dog, a meek dog, cringing for my meat,
Not for me the fireside, the well-filled plate,
But shut door, and sharp stone, and cuff and kick and hate.

Not for me the other dogs, running by my side,
Some have run a short while, but none of them would bide.
O mine is still the one trail, the hard trail, the best,
Wide wind, and wild stars, and hunger of the quest!

Full of the Moon
KARLA KUSKIN

It's full of the moon
The dogs dance out
Through brush and bush and bramble.
They howl and yowl
And growl and prowl.
They amble, ramble, scramble.
They rush through brush.
They push through bush.
They yip and yap and hurr.
They lark around and bark around
With prickles in their fur.
They two-step in the meadow.
They polka on the lawn.
Tonight's the night
The dogs dance out
And chase their tails till dawn.

Dog
VALERIE WORTH

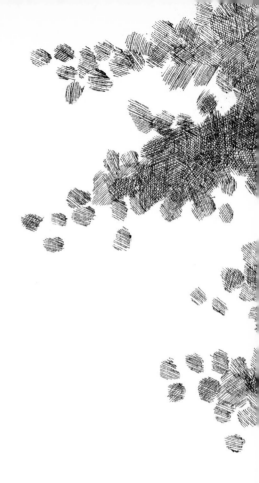

Under a maple tree
The dog lies down,
Lolls his limp
Tongue, yawns,
Rests his long chin
Carefully between
Front paws;
Looks up, alert;
Chops, with heavy
Jaws, at a slow fly,
Blinks, rolls
On his side,
Sighs, closes
His eyes: sleeps
All afternoon
In his loose skin.

24

FROM
Friend Dog
ARNOLD ADOFF

dog

    you
    are my friend
and
    i
    am your friend
dog

we are for
each
    other

    . . .

friend and dog

       because

you are both

and they
    are both the same
that
  is
 your
 name.

26

Pete at the Seashore

DON MARQUIS

i ran along the yellow sand
and made the sea gulls fly
i chased them down the waters edge
i chased them up the sky

i ran so hard i ran so fast
i left the spray behind
i chased the flying flecks of foam
and i outran the wind

an airplane sailing overhead
climbed when it heard me bark
i yelped and leapt right at the sun
until the sky grew dark

some little children on the beach
threw sticks and ran with me
o master let us go again
and play beside the sea

A Dog
CHARLOTTE ZOLOTOW

I am alone.
Someone is raking leaves
outside
and there is one yellow leaf
on the black branch
brushing the window.

Suddenly a wet cold nose
nuzzles
my empty hand.

Gone

DAVID McCORD

I've looked behind the shed
And under every bed:
I think he must be dead.

What reason for alarm?
He doesn't know the farm.
I *knew* he'd come to harm!

He was a city one
Who never had begun
To think the city fun.

Now where could he have got?
He doesn't know a lot.
I haven't heard a shot.

That old abandoned well,
I thought. Perhaps he fell?
He didn't. I could tell.

Perhaps he found a scent:
A rabbit. Off he went.
He'll come back home all spent.

Groundhogs, they say, can fight;
And raccoons will at night.
He'd not know one by sight!

I've called and called his name.
I'll never be the same.
I blame myself . . . I blame . . .

All *he* knows is the park;
And now it's growing dark.
A bark? *You hear a bark?*

Familiar Friends

JAMES S. TIPPETT

The horses, the pigs,
And the chickens,
The turkeys, the ducks
And the sheep!
I can see all my friends
From my window
As soon as I waken
From sleep.

The cat on the fence
Is out walking.
The geese have gone down
For a swim.
The pony comes trotting
Right up to the gate;
He knows I have candy
For him.

The cows in the pasture
Are switching
Their tails to keep off
The flies.
And the old mother dog
Has come out in the yard
With five pups to give me
A surprise.

Old Dog

PATRICIA HUBBELL

Old dog! Old dog!
Why do you hold your paw so?
Why do you curl your lip so?
Do your pads remember the running rabbits, the
                                 whirring partridge?

Is it dreams, old dog, that make you shudder so?
Smell dreams descending to your paws and giving them
                                     the twitch?

Is it that or something new, old dog?
Some unknown, unsuspected smell filling up the night
and your distended nostrils?

You cannot shun it now, old dog. Your nose was
meant for smells.

Breathe deep. Breathe deep.

The Prayer of the Dog

CARMEN BERNOS DE GASZTOLD

Lord,
I keep watch!
If I am not here
who will guard their house?
Watch over their sheep?
Be faithful?
No one but You and I
understands
what faithfulness is.
They call me, "Good dog! Nice dog!"
Words . . .
I take their pats
and the old bones they throw me
and I seem pleased.
They really believe they make me happy.
I take kicks too
when they come my way.
None of that matters.
I keep watch!
Lord,
do not let me die
until, for them,
all danger is driven away.

      Amen

FROM
The Old Dog's Song
LESLIE NORRIS

All night I've kept an eye
Open protectingly
In case of danger.
If anything had gone wrong,
I would have raised my strong
Voice in anger.
But all was safe and still.
The sun's coming over the hill,
No need for warning.
When he comes down the stair
I shall be waiting there
To say Good Morning.

The Span of Life

ROBERT FROST

The old dog barks backward without getting up.
I can remember when he was a pup.

For Mugs

MYRA COHN LIVINGSTON

He is gone now. He is dead.
There is a hurting in my head.

I listen for his bark, his whine.
The silence answers. He was mine.

I taught him all the greatest tricks.
I had a way of throwing sticks

So he could catch them, and a ball
We bounced against the backyard wall.

I can see him, chasing cats,
Killing all the mountain rats,

Drinking water from his bowl.
There's a place he had a hole

To bury bones, but now it's gone.
His footprints fade upon the lawn.

He used to snuggle on my bed
But now he's gone. He died. He's dead.

FROM
The Seasons

Autumn
HARRY BEHN

Across cold, moon-bright
distant stillness, a dog barks,
and then another.

Index

OF AUTHORS,
TITLES, AND
FIRST LINES